INSIDE THE ADOLESCENT ALCOHOLIC

INSIDE THE ADOLESCENT ALCOHOLIC

by

Ann Marie Krupski

First published September, 1982

I.S.B.N. 0-89486-159-X

Printed in the United States of America.

CONTENTS

PREFACE

When I was a seasoned music educator for students in grades kindergarten through eighth, I became sensitized to the joys and traumas of childhood and adolescence. For some reason, I was especially touched by the struggles of adolescents. Sometimes they were moody, sometimes disruptive and sometimes courteous and attentive. Almost always I was aware of their heightened self-consciousness and their unwanted awkwardness.

After I received training in alcoholism counseling, I became even more aware of the role that alcohol plays in adolescents' lives. Many times I discovered that the very adolescents who were most annoying or disruptive or withdrawn were those who were living with an actively abusing alcoholic parent or an actively abusing sibling. Often I discovered that they, themselves, had begun to experiment with alcohol.

In my years of teaching, adolescent disruptive behavior often became very distracting to the educating process. Such distraction was so disturbing that I lost sight of the multiple causes of the behavior. I *only* knew the frustration of disruptions and the challenge of getting the attention of high energy adolescents.

In my work as an alcoholism counselor, I have become more aware of acute tensions in many adolescents. Although I still experience frustration because of resistance and manipulative behavior, I also have learned to go beyond the behaviors to the pain. Years after my days as a teacher, adolescents finally have been able to teach *me*. What I write here represents pieces of what I have learned from adolescent alcoholics and their parents.

Under ordinary circumstances, adolescence is as vulnerable a time as any other developmental period. Under ordinary circumstances, the adolescent experiences frequent oscillations of self-esteem, heightened self-absorption, extreme touchiness and ambivalence about reliance on or repudiation of parental support. Once an adolescent becomes addicted to alcohol, no circumstances remain ordinary. The distress of adolescence is accentuated and distorted in a whirlwind of alcohol-induced confusion.

In the mysterious process of counseling, I enter the private space of many adolescents' intra-psychic worlds. I enter a space from which they themselves too often try to escape. At times, I, too, want to escape. I find much darkness in many adolescents' inner worlds. I find a great reservoir of unexpressed personal anguish. And despite any external gruffness, I continue to find great sensitivity. Despite any rude mannerisms, I continue to find tenderness wrapped in much fear.

When I first began to write *Inside the Adolescent Alcoholic*, I wrote in order to record my own thoughts. My writing was a way for me to reflect on a very painful experience with one female adolescent. In reflecting on one adolescent I was able to define more clearly my experiences with the many adolescent alcoholics with whom I work. My writing gave me the needed space to make concrete what I have learned about adolescent alcoholics and their parents. As I wrote, I realized that I had been entering the darkest regions of the adolescent's heart. I was able to identify more firmly what goes on inside the adolescent alcoholic. And I identified not only their pain but also my own hopes for their movement toward freedom from the anguish of addiction.

My experiences with adolescents are exhilirating and draining. In my most discouraging moments, I question if recovery is possible for anyone in this developmental period. Yet when an adolescent begins sobriety or achieves insight, I breathe a sigh of relief and offer myself words of encouragement. And so, I write because of the encouragement adolescent alcoholics in recovery give me.

It is my hope that what I have written will touch your heart; for I mean to speak to your heart. If you are a teacher, parent, counselor or mental health professional, it is helpful for you to know the darkest regions of the adolescent's experience.

If this work makes a contribution, I hope that it is in the area of touching hearts and lifting the veil of false preconceptions about the adolescent alcoholic. It is my hope that this work will enable you to perceive in depth the adolescent alcoholic's intra-psychic world. Perhaps you will then understand more about the consuming anguish and the destructive behaviors which flow from the unresolved pain of addiction. Perhaps, too, you will be touched by the parallel struggles of the parents.

It is important to point out that I will not offer you techniques of approach with the adolescent. This material is not meant to serve as a manual. My purpose is to describe adolescent alcoholics' behavior and pain and that of their parents. For the most part, I have limited myself to a description of one adolescent alcoholic's intra-psychic world. My intention is to help you really see *inside* the adolescent alcoholic.

July, 1982
Ann Marie Krupski

INTRODUCTION

Because my discussion of the addicted adolescent in therapy was inspired by a young woman, all of my observations are written in the feminine gender; however, they are just as valid for addicted male adolescents. By "adolescents," I am speaking of persons through 24 years of age.

In keeping with laws of confidentiality, the names I use and also some incidental details are fictitious. The seriousness of Debbie's stage of addiction and all other facts are true.

It is my hope that the observations I offer will serve as reassuring support to counselors, educators, or parents, and that these observations will also afford some insight to those concerned about their own or another's use of alcohol. Those of you whose journey through life has somewhat paralleled that of the young woman I write about will find this to be your story, too.

I conclude with one last observation. It would be not only simplistic, but also irreverant, to generalize about what to expect when an adolescent alcoholic enters therapy. Truly, it is not possible to simplify any unique human story. What the following story represents is indeed a universal experience which genuinely reflects the condition of adolescents who have alcoholism, and especially those who are in treatment for alcoholism.

PART ONE

SHE HAS ALCOHOLISM

As I turned into the driveway of the large neatly-kept house with the carefully landscaped yard, my heart pounded, and I continued to rebel against being there. Although I didn't want to get out of the car, I did, and the door closed behind me with a slam. Only the clear, crisp tranquillity of this late fall day sustained me. I hesitantly approached the front door, rang the doorbell, and waited.

My attention turned to the misgivings I had. I wanted to close my mind to these disturbing thoughts, but a myriad of considerations went on and on in my head. If only I didn't have to say why I had come. If only someone else could do this. If only they would understand. If only she could appreciate what I was doing. As I approached this necessary, but difficult, task all my "if only's" multiplied into infinity.

The door was opened by the vibrant, attractive 18-year-old woman I had come to see, and the gracious greeting I received made me even more uncomfortable. When I met her mother, however, I knew that any diversionary attempt would be not only impossible but also unjust. And so, I entered into the warmth of a home where my initial warm reception would soon turn cold.

We moved into the richly decorated living room. The clear, quiet music of an FM radio station provided the background accompaniment for our initial exchanges and pleasantries. My personal discomfort, however, was not alleviated. What had to be shared, had to be said. Despite my own resistance, I began.

1

"I am going to tell you something that Debbie does not want me to say, but I have to tell you. You must know." My speech became subdued, and I forced each word "Debbie — has — alcoholism." Silence descended like a dark cloud. Yet, I knew I had to continue: "Somehow the addictive process has started in her and is already well established."

The room was filled with the static of a sudden, staggering, unforeseen shock. Mrs. Albertson sat rigidly in her stiff chair. Debbie's eyes remained fixed. As I continued, time dissolved in the darkness of my unfolding message. Debbie, uneasy yet determined, interrupted, "You're wrong. I am not one! I'm not an alcoholic." With tear-filled eyes and an expression of surprise, Mrs. Albertson asked if they could get a second opinion.

Just then a car door slammed, and Mrs. Albertson left the room to see who had arrived. Debbie and I were alone. Her hurt and angry looks were disquieting. She said, "I thought you weren't going to tell her." In an irritated and obstinate tone she added, "That makes you a liar then. You're a *liar*." The words echoed in my ears and burned deep down inside of me. The only words I could say were "I had no choice, Debbie. I just had no choice."

When Mrs. Albertson reentered the room, she introduced me to her husband. My legs trembled as I rose and extended my hand. For I knew that the interrupted discussion was about to continue where we had left off and would include this important family member. The pain of what had been said was reemphasized upon repetition. The words which had filled the room and shaken hearts were uttered again. Although it was obvious that Mrs. Albertson felt more secure with her husband present, the intensity of my message gained momentum, and three of us broke down and cried. The ensuing silence surrounded us. These moments were pregnant with attentive and concerned participation. Mr. Albertson's stern visage provided a striking contrast to the previous emotional scene. However, after what seemed to be an excruciatingly long deliberation, he said, "I'm not happy about your assessment, but also, I am not really surprised."

PART TWO

THE DIAGNOSIS

I share this much of the Albertsons' story with you because it impacted my professional development. In fact, it is the starting point of my subsequent observations about Debbie's course of treatment for alcoholism.

This revealing vignette is singular only to the extent that it portrays an occurrence within the context of a home visit. Such a visitation outside the agency was necessary because of Debbie's home confinement while recovering from mononucleosis. Sadly enough, the escalation of adolescent addiction to alcohol and the necessity for sharing assessments with family members is too common a situation in America today.

At this point, a reader might wonder how a diagnosis of alcohol addiction is determined for an adolescent. Although it is not the intent here to elaborate on that detailed clinical process, I will mention some necessary information. Because addiction to alcohol is a disease, it not only has a progression which ends with death if left untreated, but also has presenting symptoms. Most of us have little knowledge of the addictive process and even less awareness of the observable symptomatology of the various stages of addiction in adults. Moreover, few of us are conscious of any presenting early symptoms of addiction in adolescents. We are more inclined to recognize that a person is addicted only when the addiction is well established; when it is apparent to anyone who is acquainted with the adolescent. The person's behavior at this point becomes intolerable, and glaring physical and/or legal problems have resulted from alcohol abuse.

In Debbie's case, I did not have to labor over a diagnosis. Her symptomatology was too apparent, for she was already into an advanced stage of addiction. She had experienced physical, psychological, social, and legal disruption as a result of her drinking. For instance, some of her presenting symptoms were:

— blackouts or alcohol-induced amnesia

— unplanned periods of intoxication

— regular, heavy drinking

— three "driving under the influence" arrests within six months

— expressed parental concern

— slight hand tremors upon withdrawal from alcohol

— lack of interest in activities not associated with drinking coupled with an inability to hold a job.

In order to meaningfully journey with the Albertsons as they experience Debbie's addiction, it is my intent to focus not only on Debbie's, but also on her parents' reaction to and acceptance of her addiction. Some of the reasons which necessitate such a dual reflection are:

— As a chemically dependent adolescent, whether in the process of recovery or not, Debbie has a tremendous impact on those around her.

— The stages through which Debbie progresses will be paralleled by her parents.

— Each parent has been affected by much of Debbie's dysfunctional behavior, and each somehow has adapted or maladapted to her behavior.

— As Debbie embarks upon recovery, her parents can provide a vital support role in the recovery process.

In the course of my clinical practice with those who have alcoholism, I have observed that there is a striking similarity between the adolescent's reaction to her own alcoholism and the reactions of dying patients to their terminal illnesses. In Elisabeth Kubler-Ross's book, *On Death and Dying*, she describes the coping mechanisms used by those with terminal illnesses. These coping mechanisms are described as the five stages which people often go through when faced with their own death. These stages serve as a basis for my own observations about the adolescent's and the parents' reactions to a diagnosis of alcoholism. The five stages are denial, anger, bargaining, depression, and acceptance. These stages will be illustrated as the Albertsons discover and learn about chemical dependency.

As we examine these stages in theory, stage identification seems to flow neatly and logically, and each stage and its components are understandable. In actual circumstances, very few persons proceed from stage to stage in such an orderly, well-defined manner. Unfortunately, reality is not all that neat. Although there definitely are commonalities from person to person and family to family, there also are distinct and out-of-the-established-order differences. For example, there are times when a person can simultaneously exhibit various aspects of two or more stages or even completely skip a stage.

First Stage: DENIAL

While denial functions as a buffer to block out overwhelming anxiety, it also enables Debbie and her parents to reject reality on many separate occasions. To be addicted to alcohol is one issue, but to be addicted and only eighteen is quite another.

Even a trained counselor must resist the inclination to close one's eyes to the reality of an adolescent's addiction.

Initially, I was a bit too ready to support Debbie's denial. At some point in time, however, I faced a twofold reality:

(1) determining that the addictive process had been established in Debbie; and

(2) sharing that assessment not only with Debbie, but also with her parents.

It is common that the adolescent or at least one of the parents will reject the reality of addiction. The human mechanism almost instinctively allows for this initial delusion. Most of us do not easily sustain the temporary disorientation and concomitant insecurity evoked by new, unpleasant information. Initially, obvious and crushing anxiety will become blatant denial. As shown in the vignette, Debbie responded to the assessment of her addiction with, "You're wrong, I am not one! I'm not an alcoholic." Her mother, on the other hand, asked if they could get a second opinion. Very often, thereafter, a simmering almost unconscious agony is manifested in more subtle dynamics. Either Debbie will continue to drink, or she will cut down on her drinking, or she will stop completely for a short period (or even for a period of several weeks) but continue to go out with her same drinking friends. She may even get a job as a bartender and give all kinds of teetotaler advice to her customers and her friends.

One or both of the parents will probably not support counseling and will make negative comments about the process or the counselor. They might not provide transportation. They will not talk to the adolescent or to each other about what is happening. If they do talk with the adolescent, they will want to give credence to *all* that might be related defensively. They will want to focus on several possibilities other than alcohol as the cause of the adolescent's present situation. Such considered alternative possibilities often include the "if onlys": she had a different job; she had different friends; we didn't pressure her so much; she could settle down; we had not moved to this neighborhood; she was not immature; the counselor was not so biased.

Debbie and her parents can be expected to reject the reality of her alcoholism again and again. Some rejections of this reality are blatant; others are less obvious. The experienced counselor knows this and neither discounts denial nor immediately breaks through it, but rather carefully monitors, consistently respects and therapeutically uses it so that the adolescent and her parents can grow in their ability to consider, recognize, and accept a reality which initially was too frightening.

SECOND STAGE: ANGER

In the face of an assessment of chemical dependency, anger is an honest human emotion. Although Debbie might hesitate to welcome its intensity, anger will envelop her in a stance which mingles resentment, rebellion, antagonism, and extreme anxiety.

A roar of indignation will rise in the heart of an adolescent whose belief system has been shaped by myths. Debbie's resentment comes as no surprise when we realize that her concept of an alcoholic is that of the stereotypic, degenerate skid row bum. Within her conceptual framework, the word alcoholic conjures up only this one vivid, repugnant picture. How can anyone identify her with that which is so repulsive? Debbie knows she is not one of *those* people. She resents this assault on her self-esteem. Because she perceives the counselor as offensive, her accumulating anger generates a colossal fury.

At first, Debbie was unable to vent her anger. To suppress her anger would have been unhealthy, for if repressed, rage simmers and the smoldering embers eventually flame into delayed or indirect expressions. Debbie might either feel anger as a delayed reaction or as a wish for revenge. She might rebel by becoming a passive participant in violence through television or in books. She might even begin to misperceive other persons as angry and become righteously indignant as a defense against them. Therefore, it is a beneficial experience when an adolescent is able to express anger.

Because parents share a similar mythology of addiction, the roar of indignation will be as disquieting to them. The myths which Mr. and Mrs. Albertson maintain are also shaped by the media and reaffirmed by other acquaintances whose belief systems have been molded by cultural myths.

Initially, there may be obvious signs that Debbie and/or her parents are enraged for they see the counselor's assessment of alcohol addiction and their own stereotypic concepts of it as incompatible. Such a discrepancy of views builds tension that will immediately be discharged in displacement. For the most part, the counselor will be the recipient of verbal and/or physical displays of outrage; i.e., walking out of the room, slamming the door, pounding a piece of furniture, yelling and cursing. There can also be more obscure, almost concealed, indications that the parents are angry. Some manifestations of anger are not direct. Anger wears many masks, some of which are easily recognizable, some are not.

If the Albertsons feel angry about the assessment but do not express it, the anger will not be eliminated but converted to alternate, camouflaged expressions. Some of these expressions might include:

(1) *Infuriating Deliberations*
Debbie and her parents might experience infuriating,

distracting thoughts and emotions which need to be brought up and addressed as common, understandable occurrences. Upon recognition, the reappearance of these inevitable thoughts will become infrequent. If they do reoccur, they usually do so with less intensity. Let me give some examples:

Parents' deliberations: What kind of parents does that counselor think we are? Who does she think she is? Doesn't she know our background? She must need more clients. She doesn't know what she's talking about. We've done everything for this child.

Debbie's deliberations: It's a pain in the neck to come to this place. I have better things to do with my time. I'm not going to miss any work in order to keep an appointment. I'm not as bad as she thinks. She should see some of my friends when they drink. All she does is sit in an office. She doesn't know what's really going on out there.

(2) *Subtle Belittlement of Therapy*

As long as a hostile impulse exists, indirect manifestations of anger will continue. At some point, it can be expected that an adolescent will inconspicuously minimize the serious task of therapy. An adolescent will either exaggerate or misquote a statement made by the counselor, over-dramatize selected portions of a session, or mimic some of the techniques utilized. She may come late for an appointment or capitalize on any imperfections of the counselor. If not done during a counseling session, this subtle belittlement will be done in the parents' presence. Therefore, what needs to be remembered is that an adolescent's derisive portrayal of a counseling session necessarily will distort the parents' view of the therapeutic process.

(3) *Parental Sabotage*

If such a distortion develops, the parents can easily contribute to a sabotage of treatment. They will either condone the adolescent's portrayal or, if possible, terminate the counseling, ask for a new counselor, or refuse to attend any meetings with the counselor. This dynamic emphasizes the need for involving parents in the treatment process at the beginning of therapy.

(4) *Consistent Reluctance to Talk*

Because of the adolescent's normal distrust of adults, it can be expected that anger will contribute to a reluctance to talk about herself, her drinking or her life history. This reluctance may be as exaggerated as silence in response to a question, as seemingly insignificant as monosyllabic responses, or as annoying as avoidance through attempts to change the subject.

(5) *Glaring Statements of Disgruntlement*

A blatant expression of grievances will be aired early in therapy, especially by adolescents coerced into the program by a court, school principal, or drinking and driving program. Since the adolescen initially feels mistreated, anger will often be externalized in expressions such as:

— The principal and I never got along. He never did like me.
— They never showed me the results of the breathalyzer test. They probably made up the results.
— There were other kids involved, but they singled me out.
— This whole mess is stupid. I don't see why I should be punished when I don't even have a drinking problem.
— This is ridiculous. It's the first time I ever made a mistake like this.

— You can't make me stop drinking, so don't bother trying. If I want to drink, I will — no matter what you say.

As long as the adolescent participates in covert manifestations of anger, she is externalizing the anger to protect herself from facing realities within herself. If she cannot attach the blame to her counselor or her parents or the police or anyone or anything else, she will be forced to blame only herself. The subsequent feelings of guilt and self-reproach will be painful and, initially, all too overpowering. When Debbie's depression is discussed in stage four, a prime focus will be her experience of self-blame and guilt.

Third Stage: BARGAINING

During adolescence, the young adult experiences a heightened sense of omnipotence which is exercised as repeatedly as possible and as consistently as conceivable. Because of a high level of volatile physical energy, the adolescent struggles to utilize substantial and sometimes clumsy expressions of power and autonomy. Very often, such expressions become evident in overt or subtle manipulations. Such manipulations, frequently in the form of bargaining maneuvers, are an attempt to consciously or unconsciously exercise psychological control of another person. Moreover, the bargaining terms utilized are often concealed. They can be hidden in the delicate shadows and the awkward, adaptive nuances of the adolescent's communications with us.

Within a therapeutic framework, the counselor can expect to be a target of the young adolescent's power struggle with adults. For it is within this very setting that the adolescent's sense of omnipotence is threatened. For instance, when any of the counselor's interactions with the adolescent are perceived as threatening her delusions, the adolescent almost unconsciously selects bargaining as an adaptive exercise of her ego strength. Even subtle forms of bargaining begin to be practiced with an almost desperate abandon and determined emphasis. Although an underlying theme of the bargaining efforts is the manipulation for power, the variations of such efforts are as unique as the individual involved. Therefore, once we recognize the main theme, we learn to identify even the less elaborate variations.

As we consider the bargaining maneuvers used by the adolescent, it is important to remember that any and all such manipulative schemes flow from a perceived threat to the adolescent's delusions of indestructability. Such maneuvers also draw upon an unconscious, adaptive exercise of ego strength. As a result, therefore, the adolescent employs all possible efforts to revise the reality of her situation in a way which deceives the counselor. Repeated and cunning attempts are made not only to exercise the strong, persistent feelings of omnipotence but also to reinforce the adolescent's inflexible belief of having the magical ability to control an adult's response to any of her actions.

In summation, the underlying framework and precursors to bargaining include:

(1) the adolescent's delusion of indestructability, a heightened sense of omnipotence

(2) resistance by a seeming revision of reality — giving the appearance that a change has been made when, in fact, that is not the case

(3) the fantasy of being able to control another person, especially an adult

(4) an unconscious, adaptive exercise of ego strength.

Bargaining Maneuvers:

It is a fascinating phenomenon to witness and to work with an adolescent who has been referred for assessment by the court or by the probation department. Although some adolescents are a bit disgruntled in the initial phases of assessment, they also are cooperative with the procedure. However, if a court referral for ongoing, outpatient counseling is mandated in lieu of a jail sentence, an entirely new dynamic often results. At first, it is very easy for the inexperienced counselor to miss the subtleties of this dynamic. For what happens is often the following:

> The adolescent begins to keep appointments, a beginning relationship emerges, and the counselor perceives all of this process as good. Within a matter of weeks or months, however, *quasi-compliance* to mandated therapy can be expected. The adolescent struggles to fade into the woodwork of therapy by one of many methods. She may keep appointments but not cooperate with the counselor at any level of significance; she may begin to keep intermittent appointments, sometimes with a phone call to reschedule. At other times, however, the counselor has to notify the adolescent or the court that an appointment has been missed; the adolescent simply skips two or more consecutive appointments and then returns; the adolescent geographically escapes by enlisting in a branch of the armed service, by working long hours out of town or by moving to a new, unknown address or by actually moving from the area.

When *quasi-compliance* with therapy occurs, it becomes clear that the underlying motivation has been to stay out of jail. The impending thoughts of regimented confinement cause psychological discomfort. Initial acceptance of the court mandate for therapy in lieu of detention rapidly deteriorates into a blatant attempt to postpone the focus on a drinking problem. In a sense, the adolescent has promised to go to counseling in exchange for freedom.

Once counseling begins, the terms of the bargain are no longer agreeable to the adolescent. At the time of the court decision, the problem was not drinking, but fear of confinement. Because the adolescent experiences some sense of relief and triumph about having escaped restrictions of incarceration, she decides unwittingly and incisively to nullify treatment. Treatment has no meaning to someone who perceives no personal problem other than the persistence of a determined counselor. If, however, the counselor is able to keep the adolescent in outpatient treatment, other manipulative maneuvers can be expected to replace quasi-compliance. The adolescent has an uncanny talent to repeatedly attempt to outwit any unsuspecting adult. Until this manipulative attitude is modified, the adolescent perseveres in a determined attempt to achieve the result she considers to be most advantageous.

Because the adolescent has an urgent need to allay any feelings of guilt, *promises to stop* are made not only to self but also to others. Such promises ordinarily are made from sincerity and self-recrimination. They are also aimed at keeping counselors and/or parents quiet. In other words, "Bug off. Get off my back." Although these promises cannot be treated disrespectfully, neither can they be honored as magnificent blessings nor as long-lasting solutions for anyone involved. Firm resolutions to reform which do not have real commitment are unconscious manipulations to ease external, parental and/or other expressed discontent. If the promises are accepted by adults, the adolescent also believes she has gained some control over the adults. The promises initially do relieve parental and/or other pressure; however, all too often, the relief is only temporary. As soon as the drinking resumes, self-guilt reemerges and external pressure resumes.

Another variation of a *promise to stop* is often exercised by the adolescent. It is translated as "I can quit any time. Some day I'll stop drinking, but not now." This type of promise is an attempt to postpone all that could be involved in abstention. Rationalizations enable the adolescent to persist in postponing sobriety. For example, "I'm too young; everyone my age drinks. I like to drink. It hasn't hurt me or anyone else, so far."

The adolescent makes major and commendable efforts through *controlled drinking* to prove that she has no problem with alcohol. For those who are in an early or early middle stage of addiction to alcohol, it is a common effort to abstain completely for several weeks. Again because of individual variations, some adolescents totally abstain, some "cut down" on their intake, some substitute other drugs for drinking, and some cut down on drinking while maintaining a level of other drug usage. If any of these efforts are used, the adolescent will frequently express her position as follows:

> I haven't been drunk or had a drink since the night of my arrest. If I were an alcoholic, I wouldn't be able to do that. See, I really don't have a problem with alcohol. I don't even need a drink, you're all wrong about me.

This partially convincing attempt to persuade the counselor that there is no problem is a subtle, but clever, form of psychological blackmail. The implied translation of the message becomes:

> I have improved and therefore deserve a reward from you, my counselor. Coming here and talking to you hasn't helped a bit. I stopped (or cut down) drinking on my own. Since I don't have a problem anyway, this counseling stuff really is dumb.

Come on now, you can dismiss me. I don't have to keep seeing you anymore, do I?

A counselor cannot too readily trust any messages similar to the above and needs to be ready not only to recognize, but also to frustrate the adolescent's efforts to control. At the same time, the counselor can expect to be the recipient of the adolescent's outstanding flare for provocation. Moreover, the counselor also needs to recognize and be ready to respond to the situation in which she finds herself.

At times, when we can afford a few moments for laughter, and when we can be somewhat objective, we sense and enjoy the more humorous aspects of working with someone who is in a power struggle with us. When working with an adolescent, we need to be constantly alert. For the adolescent deliberately and/or instinctively struggles to elicit our support by *tricking* us into a transaction whose cousin could very well be extortion. The ability to make deals of any kind is a distinguishing quality of the adolescent's illusion of power. She expects us to cater to her whims as if they were our own. Furthermore, the adolescent repeatedly and with extraordinary agility strives to *trick* us into making mutual deals. The terms of the propositions ordinarily are clear, but the small print is buried in the heart of the adolescent's communication with us.

The adolescent typically inclines to a few patterns when making deals or *tricky transactions*. Examples of which are:

— The only time I can make appointments is after 6:00 p.m. See me then or not at all.

— If you contacted the Department of Motor Vehicles and told them how good I'm doing, I could get my license back. Then I would be able to make my appointments here.

— Look, I just graduated from high school. Why don't you release me as a present?

18

— Hey, listen. You have to give me another appointment because I have to go to my cousin's wedding.

— If I call you, that should be enough. I called you the last four times, so even if I haven't been to the agency, at least I've talked to you. That *should* be enough.

— If you send a letter to the Judge, I might be able to get out of jail. Then you wouldn't have to visit me here.

Of course, the implied translation of any deal-making transaction is: Give me any freedom, and I'll let you feel as if you really have helped me. After all, being a counselor, you probably would like to feel as if you have helped me. So here's your chance.

The counselor cannot risk participating in adolescent-initiated propositions, for repetitious resistance to the adolescent's obstinate haggling can be therapeutic. The adolescent needs to learn that the counselor's decisions regarding her welfare do not hinge on an alliance with her narcissism.

As a counselor continues to work with an adolescent, unrelenting vigilance is vital to the process. The counselor needs to be sharply aware of the adolescent's strong and tenacious reliance on such a seemingly primitive mechanism as *seduction with charm*. Some adolescents give us highly complimentary and reiterated messages which are intended to distract us from the work of therapy. For instance:

— You really are helping me.

— I feel so much better after we've talked.

— I'm glad I got you and not that other counselor. You're really okay with me.

— Since I've been talking to you, even my teachers see a difference in me.

— You're one of the few people I can talk to.

19

— You seem to understand me.

— You're not as mean as I thought you were going to be.

— Since I've been seeing you, I have tried to cut down on my drinking.

— I can tell you're a good counselor. I've been to shrinks before. But your eyes really look right into me.

When it is obvious that the adolescent is frequently attempting to allure us with flattery, it can be noted that she is acting on the fantasy that even though she is in treatment there really is no treatment. Again, the adolescent continues to make every attempt possible to invalidate the therapeutic process. Thereby, she exercises a fundamental resistance to treatment.

Very often, while the adolescent attempts to seduce the counselor with charm, she also attempts to dissuade her parents from support of the therapeutic process. While the counselor receives engaging compliments, the parents, too, fall under the influence of adolescent charm. The process with the parents can happen in one of many ways. The adolescent begins to discuss "openly" with the parents what is happening in counseling. Many parents are delighted by the adolescent's apparent willingness to confide in them. However, what actually occurs is that the adolescent attempts to improve her own relative position by degradation of her opponent. Therefore, parents receive messages about the counselor which, in a sense, they initially endorse. For an obvious put-down of the counselor appears to be an affirmation of their own position with the adolescent. If the parents succumb to this variation of *seduction with charm*, then they, too, come to believe that the counselor is of no help to the adolescent. When parents support the adolescent's fundamental resistance to treatment with "this particular counselor," they readily subscribe to termination of treatment, to the selection of a new counselor, or to transfer to a different treatment facility.

The previous considerations not only describe but also reemphasize the adolescent's finesse in bargaining. Any of these manipulative efforts are not relinquished easily; they are a defense for conquering the adult and avoiding change. However, each adolescent does not make use of all of these bargaining manuevers. Some adolescents have an extensive and well-refined repertoire which is used with much regularity; while others make tenuous, awkward attempts at such mastery; and still others exercise infrequent efforts at bargaining. Furthermore, it is significant to note that the adolescent's level of proficiency in using manipulative schemes is correlated directly with the stage of addiction to alcohol. Those in more advanced stages of addiction appear to be not only more skilled, more cunning, and more practiced in their execution of bargaining maneuvers but also more desperate and more determined in their expressions of a restricted, stifled sense of power and autonomy.

Fourth Stage: DEPRESSION

Passage through adolescence involves much insecurity, deep searching, fear, and incoherence. Because self-identity is in the process of development, the adolescent has few, internalized, stable points of reference. The inner world of the adolescent almost daily assumes a new, unsettling shape. Anguish caused by the disorientation of profound physical and psychological changes is compounded when the adolescent becomes addicted to any chemical substance. For addiction distorts and aborts the adolescent's experience of the self.

Moreover, once an adolescent becomes addicted, self-blame and a sense of loss invade the already tumultuous terrain of the adolescent's inner world, and the ordinary but unsettling turmoil of adolescence is exaggerated even more. At this point, depression follows the self-blame and sense of loss. Thereafter, the depression accompanies the complexity of addiction. The adolescent often becomes a short-fused, unpredictable time bomb ready to explode without provocation. And if not ready to explode, the adolescent withdraws into a protective, but isolating, shell of loneliness.

And so Debbie was a veritable, detonated dynamite keg in my office. Although she may have suffered some minimal depression before she became addicted, depression was a secondary symptom which did not predate the addiction but rather resulted from it. Debbie experienced the self-blame and sense of loss which trigger and accompany depression.

It is important to realize that the multiple dynamics operative with Debbie are also paralleled in family members. Denial, anger, bargaining, and depression, which of necessity are described separately, can interplay with each other, can occur simultaneously, or can occur in rapid succession or less rapid progression — one after the other. No matter how these patterns of behavior present themselves in the adolescent, the experience of these multiple dynamics still remains that of a debilitating onslaught. Among some factors which affect the intensity of the onslaught are: personality, stage of addiction, stage of recovery, and accessibility of familial and/or professional support.

Because so many dynamics interplay within the adolescent, the depression may not surface immediately. Or if it does occur early in treatment, it may be overshadowed by other more apparent and more annoying behaviors. Be that as it may, both the parents and the adolescent will experience some degree of depression.

The *self-blame* that Debbie aimed against herself was related directly to her drinking. The following statement emanated from her self-blame:

— I shouldn't have gone to that bar.
— What's wrong with me? I was only going to have two beers. I was so stupid last night.
— What a fool I was.
— If I didn't get drunk, I wouldn't have had that accident.
— I shouldn't have had so much.
— I don't know why this happens to me.
— Why did I drink so much? I *am* dumb. I just can't handle booze.

On the other hand, parents can make statements such as the following:

— What did we do wrong?
— We've tried everything with this child. What more could we have done?
— What a failure we've been.
— We thought we raised this child well.
— Maybe we were too strict.
— We shouldn't have asked where she was going.
— We should have given fewer privileges.
— We should have talked with her more often.
— We should have consulted with a psychologist or with somebody, anybody.

Derogatory self-statements abound, the "shoulds" prevail. Confusion reigns. And depression works its havoc.

23

Just as is the case with denial, anger and bargaining maneuvers, the severity of the self-blame manifested is correlated directly to the stage of alcoholism. The key words here are *self-blame manifested*. Self-blame is operative in all stages of addiction — early to late. However, it is expressed more clearly in the earlier stages of addiction. For example, the adolescent might state:

— I shouldn't have had so much. I'll watch out next time.
— I was foolish and won't drink so much again.
— I wrecked my car. I never would do that if I were sober. No way am I gonna drink and drive again.
— I should have paid more attention to how much I was drinking.
— I was really dumb. It was my own stupidity — my own fault. I do things backwards anyway.

Because the expressive style of the adolescent is one of overstatement, self-blame often is stated in the midst of glaring absolutes. For instance:

— I *always* drink too much.
— I'll *never* do that again.

Self-blame becomes more entrenched the more severe the addiction. In later stages of addiction an accumulation of unexpressed self-blame burrows itself into the unconscious. It seems as if self-blame not only becomes inaccessible to the addicted person but also is converted into unconscious projectionary statements. Adolescent thought processes become even more mangled:

Others are to blame. I keep trying to do well but they're not helping me. They pressure me too much. If only they wouldn't expect so much of me. Don't they know that everybody drinks? What do they care anyway? They don't even understand me. Besides I only drink to get away from them.

24

Even drinking situations become the target of the
adolescent's projections of self-blame.

— They kept filling my glass.
— Everybody was drinking so much; I had to drink along with
them. I would have looked stupid if I didn't drink.
— I usually don't go with *that* crowd. I always get drunk when
I'm with them.
— Besides, everybody drinks more than I do. *They* should be in
counseling — not me.

As the addiction progresses, depression cuts more and
more deeply into the provisional selfhood of the adolescent.
Reality becomes more and more distorted. Isolation is
emphasized. The weight of the resultant gloom is
practically unbearable.

The depression which results from the adolescent's
almost constant bombardment of the self with blame is
wearing. Moreover, the depression is intensified by the
adolescent's sense of loss. In the course of human
development, the adolescent has reached a stage when
delusions of indestructability, power plays and struggles for
independence are at a peak. Utilization of these dynamics
permits the adolescent to experiment with self-definition.
However, at a time when birth of the self struggles for
emergence, the burgeoning forth of responsible selfhood is
clouded and possibly destroyed by the anxiety,
dependency, and confusion that accompany addiction.

Loss of Self-Identity
The adolescent is at a critical juncture on the continuum of
becoming a person, of establishing an identity of her own.
The basic challenge of all humans for self-understanding
and self-acceptance seems heightened during this stage of
human development. However, the common course of

development is complicated by addiction. For addiction profoundly alters and severely distorts the adolescent's human experience. Addiction interrupts the ongoing development toward self-realization. The adolescent becomes more alienated from herself. The result is an acute ache and a searing emptiness. A provisional self-identity turns lethargic cartwheels in an inner world of chaos. Self-consciousness becomes confused consciousness of a non-self, a different self, an addicted self. And an addicted self is not the real self.

The adolescent, however, believes she knows who she is, and yet does not know at all. In drug-induced, altered states of consciousness she experiences herself differently. There are serious discrepancies between the non-drugged experience of self and the drugged experience. She is on a narrow and perilous bridge between reality and delusion. The lure of addiction distracts her from the adolescent's instinctive search for self actualization/realization. Because she is addicted, her transition from childhood to adulthood seems like a timid experiment aimed at cheating and destroying herself. Alcohol initially provided some ecstasies on the route. However, the monument she erected to alcohol soon became her scaffold. The few hesitant steps towards self-definition were obliterated by the false assurances of alcohol.

Once the adolescent is addicted, the search for self becomes a descent into darkness, a darkness of absence. Because the adolescent no longer is on solid ground in human development, the real self is inaccessible. Therefore, she is imprisoned. Her initial movements toward self-integration are frustrated.

Confusion about self-identity is painful and is an agony shared by most adolescents. Loss of a provisional self-identity is a tragedy and often engenders a profound, penetrating panic which branches out into despair, anxiety, and frustration. The feeling of emptiness is emphasized. Psychological impoverishment prevails. The most precious qualities of being human are blunted. The manifold complexities of adolescence have been complicated even more.

Loss of Positive Self-Regard

Addiction propels the adolescent into a continuous descent from one shattering event to the next. Positive self-regard now diminishes rapidly and tumbles into what seems to be a bottomless darkness. Self-regard is lost in a blur of inaccessibility. Moreover, at this moment, the adolescent is involved in combat with self-hatred. A self whose natural propensity is toward fulfillment and health wages battle with a self warped by self-hatred and twisted by repetitious thoughts of self-destruction. Despair is heightened by self-contempt.

Times of wholesome, unadulterated fun are no more. Seasons of carefree frolic have ceased. Moments of simple and natural refreshment are unattainable. The self to which the adolescent clings tenaciously is more illusive than real. Finally, an unspeakable horror presents itself: "Is there any escape from this dark, dismal abyss?"

Similarly, disturbing thoughts become a daily reality for parents. Tension and confusion prevail.

> "If things aren't going well, something must be wrong. If something is wrong, I must be the cause. If I am the cause, I haven't done a good job. I have failed. And if I have failed, I am no good."

FIFTH STAGE: ACCEPTANCE

It is very difficult for the adolescent to reach a stage of acceptance of alcoholism. By acceptance I mean that quality which enables the addicted adolescent not only to admit that she has alcoholism but also to stop drinking and change the poor behavior occurring with the addiction. Acceptance requires an ability to be receptive and to cooperate with the demands of reality; the reality of alcoholism and recovery from it. It is a monumental task and a difficult enough one for an adult who has some sense of self-identity, let alone for an adolescent who has provisional self-definition. I focus on the following areas: recognition and admission, barriers to acceptance and some indications of acceptance.

Recognition and Admission

Denial blocked the ready admission and recognition of the disease. For an admission of alcoholism entailed recognition of the fact that Debbie was powerless over alcohol. Such recognition challenged not only Debbie, but also her parents. And so, throughout the process of therapy, Debbie's struggle to recognize and admit that she had alcoholism became apparent. I heard statements such as the following:

— "I can't be an alcoholic because I can stop drinking any time I want to stop."
— "I don't need to drink. I don't even think about it all the time."
— "If I had a problem with alcohol, I'd do something about it. Alcohol is totally out of my mind."
— "I'm too young to have alcoholism."
— "I'm not half so bad as any of the people in the drinking/driving course I attended."
— "I don't need help. I can handle this on my own."

Parents, too, echo similar strains of nonrecognition and nonadmission. I heard such statements as:

28

— "If only she would learn to have one or two drinks."

— "We've told her not to drink so much."

— "It's that crowd she hangs around with. She's never been like this before now."

— Neither of us goes overboard with alcohol. We don't know why *she* does."

Recognition and admission of the alcoholism continued to be difficult, especially when Debbie began to compare her situation with other situations. For in order to block an admission of alcoholism, Debbie began to turn to her life experiences with alcohol and then compared her circumstances with those of her friends. Using her own criteria, she excluded herself from among those who had alcoholism. At that point, all of her defense mechanisms became operative and were aimed at blocking out the painful reality.

Let me explain how Debbie used her own life circumstances to block out recognition and admission of her own alcoholism. Frequently, Debbie made comments such as:

"I just can't see it. A lot of my friends drink more than I do, and they're not here. They're not alcoholic. Or maybe they are. But if they are, then I can't be alcoholic. I'm not as bad off as they are. Besides some of them have been in jail. I haven't.

"And I haven't been drinking as much these days anyway. An alcoholic wouldn't be able to do that. I have 3 or 4 or 5 drinks, and I stop. My friends keep drinking, but I stop. And I hardly get hangovers. At least not like some of my friends. Boy do they get sick!"

My own repetitious identification of the harmful effects of alcohol in Debbie's life did not effect a significant breakthrough leading her to recognition and admission of alcoholism. As a matter of fact, after one month of outpatient treatment, Debbie responded:

"I can't drink hard liquor anymore. I know I'm an alcoholic. That's what you wanted to hear, isn't it? Come on, can't you sign a slip and let me go? I said I know I'm an alcoholic."

This response was followed immediately by, ". . . but I won't give up drinking. I'm not going to stop."

At that point, Debbie was engaged in a struggle with the recognition and admission of alcoholism. Her responses indicated that a battle raced inside of her. And already she had begun to yield superficially to the most unwanted reality of her own alcoholism. Inside of her there lived a clamorous "NO." On the surface, however, a tiny "yes" was in its infancy. I was aware that a superficial yielding to the unwanted reality of alcoholism was neither insightful recognition, nor ready admission, nor wholehearted acceptance. The louder Debbie's lip service, the more deeply embedded were her inner doubts. Her lip service to admission of her own alcoholism indicated but a wispy willingness to please the counselor and any significant others. What a struggle for the adolescent even to recognize and admit that she has alcoholism! And recognition and admission of alcoholism are a necessary beginning to the acceptance of alcoholism.

Another aspect of Debbie's struggle was the fact that recognition, admission and acceptance of alcoholism meant that she had to come to some realization of her own powerlessness over alcohol. And what adolescent wants to know the debilitating feeling of helplessness? For at the heart of Debbie's self-experience was a conscious belief supported by an almost untenable unconscious belief of personal omnipotence. She lived in a delusion of being indestructible. We all do. Such an experience is common to all of us. For instance, we think to ourselves, "Other people might get cancer, but I will not." Age and experience ordinarily enable us to refine our own delusions of indestructability. The adolescent has neither age nor experience. And what experience the addicted adolescent does have is distorted by alcohol. So rather than refining her own perception of reality, Debbie revised reality into a misperception. Again all of her defense mechanisms were operative. Debbie's thoughts might have been expressed in the following way:

"Nothing is wrong with me. I should be able to handle alcohol. After all, I'm eighteen now. I wish this counselor would get off my back. I don't have any problem with alcohol. Okay, so I've had 3 DWI's. The cops have been out to get me from the start. Besides, the second time I was overtired and hadn't eaten anything.

That counselor probably thinks anybody who comes into her office has alcoholism. What a creep she is! I'm not gonna stop drinking anyway. She's not gonna change me 'cause I don't have a problem with alcohol. I wish she'd cool it! Besides if something were wrong with me, I would know it and would do something about it."

Indeed, it takes a long time for an adolescent to recognize and admit that she has a problem with alcohol, let alone that she has alcoholism. The mysterious breakthroughs of therapy are slow in coming. Debbie and the counselor also engaged in a longstanding seesaw type exchange. The following is an example:

Debbie —   "I can manage alcohol."

Counselor —   "The facts of what has happened to you when you drink say something different. Alcohol has gotten you into trouble."

Debbie —   "Alcohol does not have a hold on me. I can live without it."

Counselor —   "The facts say that's not so. You've had 3 DWI's, have lost jobs, have had blackouts and tremors. Alcohol has gotten you into trouble, Debbie."

31

Exchanges of this type occurred for several weeks. Sometimes they go on for months. This type of exchange externalized Debbie's internal ambivalence. She had, in fact, experienced the harmful effects of her drinking. On a surface awareness, she recognized that what the counselor said was true. That surface recognition not only stirred up much anxiety, but also disturbed an inner self which tenaciously refused to relinquish her distorted view of reality. As a result, Debbie responded with "yes, buts." In the beginning of therapy, the "but" part of the clause was much, much stronger than the "yes." Her inner self was slow to relinquish its distorted view of reality.

Recognition and admission of alcoholism are necessary steps which lead toward acceptance. In and of themselves, they are *not* acceptance of alcoholism. Admission of alcoholism is not synonymous with acceptance of alcoholism. When Debbie said: "I know I'm an alcoholic," it was obvious that she was playing a game with admission. Let me give some other examples of admission which really are not admission.

— An adolescent stops drinking but keeps associating with her heavy drinking friends.
— An adolescent "cuts down" on drinking but keeps going to keg parties.
— An adolescent stops drinking but keeps on using other drugs.
— An adolescent keeps regular appointments with her counselor and gets a job as a bartender.

In other words, the adolescent seems to be saying:

"Yes, I have a problem with alcohol *BUT*, I can handle it. And I don't even have to change much in order to handle it."

Much patience and repetitious challenging were demanded of the counselor in order to mobilize Debbie's resistant inner self. Such mobilization would permit her surface recognition of the harmful effects of alcohol to penetrate her inner resistance.

At some mysterious point in time, a surface recognition of reality and the inner resistance no longer would collide, and Debbie's arrogance would dissipate. "Yes, buts," would no longer be used. And Debbie finally would recognize and admit that she had alcoholism. Such recognition and admission were my hope. If such a breakthrough occurred, movement toward acceptance would gain momentum. Without this breakthrough, Debbie's resistance to reality would continue to function with unimpaired strength.

However, if Debbie recognized and admitted her powerlessness over alcohol, she would have leaped over only one of the hurdles en route to an acceptance of her alcoholism.

Barriers to Acceptance

Debbie's ability to listen to her life reality was practically nonexistent. It is very difficult for any one of us to attend to our life reality, let alone a woman who is in one of the most difficult developmental periods of her life. The listening process is complicated further when a woman is in an intimate and destructive relationship with alcohol.

Alcohol enabled Debbie to run away from reality. In order to really listen, she not only needed to be aware of reality but also needed to participate in it. Debbie was unable to do either. She was not even able to observe in an accurate way what was going on within herself.

It also was difficult for Debbie to face the challenges I presented, because she used only her own experience and that of her friends as the norm for making any changes. Let me explain by using an example of the loss of control phenomenon.

In her experiences with alcohol, there were times (although these were getting fewer in number) when Debbie drank "a few" and suffered no negative effects. To be able to drink and suffer no negative effects was what she longed to do. When Debbie drank and had no observable negative effects, alcohol deceived her into believing such an experience could happen again and again. And so Debbie would block out the other painful memories of her involvement with alcohol. One or two positive experiences with controlling her intake would be enough to allow her to block out past, painful memories. She became increasingly unrealistic about what was within her control. When I pointed to the difficulties alcohol had caused Debbie, she heard my message as jibberish. For she lingered in those few moments when she had seeming, but momentary, victories over alcohol.

As I indicated earlier, Debbie also gave no attention to the harmful reality of her drinking because of comparisons she made with her friends. She mused, "They drank, and they weren't in treatment. So why should she be in treatment?"

And so, she kept her appointments. She received input from the counselor. She heard but did not listen. And for many weeks, she did not listen because she could not listen. Every unpleasant reality about the harmful effects of alcohol seemed to bombard her inner, resistant self. Still she maintained her position. Alcohol remained her friend; the counselor her enemy. Debbie's distorted perception was that she continued to be victimized by the counselor and not by alcohol.

Impairment of parental capacity to listen is influenced by a few factors. I noted the following: their own drinking, their own guilt and their own comparisons of Debbie with other adolescents.

If one or both parents abuse alcohol, they will not be able to listen to and understand any input from the counselor. The counselor's diagnostic assessment makes no sense to a person whose alcohol use is as serious or more serious than the adolescent's alcohol use. As a matter of fact, the counselor's assessment is too much of a threat to a parent who has alcoholism. The counselor's assessment may cause parents to consider their own use of alcohol. Such consideration may be just too threatening. And so, if parents abuse alcohol, they will be resistant to even an informal conversation with the counselor. A type of paranoia occurs, "If the counselor diagnosed my child as alcoholic, what does she think about me?"

Guilt can also impair parental capacity to listen. When parents have a poor sense of self, they readily blame themselves for any adolescent misbehavior. In order to preserve their good feelings about themselves, they must ignore any negative comments about their offspring. If they receive negative input, they blame themselves for the adolescent's behavior. Then they feel guilty and believe they have failed in their duties. These parents, therefore, approach the counselor's messages like an ostrich. The reality of the counselor's input seems to disappear, and they no longer face feelings of guilt, blame or failure.

Some parents' capacity to listen is also limited by comparisons they make with other adolescents they know. If other adolescents have been arrested more often or have been more verbally abusive to others or have been more destructive, it becomes easier for parents to minimize their own situation. When they minimize their situation, their capacity to listen to a counselor is also minimal.

Some parents, however, have a greater capacity to listen. This capacity for attention seems to be influenced by their own level of maturity and by their own freedom from addiction to alcohol. Very often it is these parents who seek out consultation for themselves and for their offspring.

It was difficult for Debbie to experience any frustration of her life activities. Somehow her immediate world had to revolve around her. Her life plans were to develop without disturbance. Her dreams and projects were to continue without interruption. Her perception was that she was in charge of herself. She was in control of her own life. She, and only she, knew best what was good for her. It was with this mind set that Debbie approached therapy. And this mind set was complicated by her addiction to alcohol. For this arrogant, self-centered, defiant attitude was accentuated by Debbie's alcoholism. In therapy, Debbie would experience many frustrations. I focus on two; the frustration of consultation with an adult who is a professional, and the resultant challenge to change her present behavior.

Consultation with an adult professional was perceived as an intrusion into her life, an invasion of her privacy and an obstruction of her plans. Debbie was unable to appreciate the counselor's concern and the consistent challenges of her relationship with alcohol. In the early phases of treatment, Debbie adhered to her previously stated position, "I won't give up drinking. I'm not going to stop." It was obvious that Debbie perceived ongoing consultation as a frustration, a direct threat to her harmful relationship with alcohol. As a result, Debbie maintained an inflexible, inner inability to stop drinking. That is, she was unable to accept any limitations where alcohol was involved. She continued to maintain that alcohol was her friend; the counselor her enemy.

The counselor's persistent call for a halt of alcohol use was not sufficient reason for Debbie to stop drinking. Part of Debbie's frustration was her own misperception that the counselor was thrusting her into a prison. The prison for Debbie was abstinence. Abstinence meant boredom. And boredom meant depression. And so, Debbie was rigid in her position. Her drinking would not be stopped. For no counselor, no adult, would tell her how to live her life. No counselor would interfere in her relationship with alcohol. Such an interference became an intolerable frustration. Debbie had no capacity for this frustration. She *would* continue to drink. No one could stop her. At that time, her reflections might have been recorded in the following way:

> I must continue to drink. What other fun is there? Besides, adults are stuffy anyway, just sticks-in-the-mud. What do they know about my needs? I know myself best. I won't be upset like this. I won't let my freedom of choice be taken away. No one can tell me what to do.

Debbie's relationship with alcohol was essential; her relationship with a counselor was not. Almost any appointment with the counselor became anxiety provoking. In Debbie's eyes, the counselor's approach was relentless. Debbie tired of repetitious probing and consistent challenges. In her eyes, the counselor was a bore. The counselor knew too much, and the counselor knew her too well. The counselor created unnecessary roadblocks. The counselor created nothing but upset for Debbie. The counselor just got in her way.

She awaited the return of freedom. She longed to party, to have fun. But the counselor spoke of change. This nagging counselor spoke of alcohol as an enemy. Debbie was intelligent. She understood too well what change meant. Change meant that old behavior could not continue. She would have to sacrifice old behavior for new. And such a sacrifice would have to be total. How could she be expected to make such a sacrifice? She had just started to have fun. What could her life be without alcohol? Couldn't anyone understand her?

Such thoughts would eat away inside Debbie. Such thoughts would escalate her mounting frustration. Her capacity for taking frustration in stride was nearly nonexistent. She did not want to change. She had no intentions of changing and, therefore, would not change. She would show all of us how strong she was.

The Albertsons had a high tolerance for frustration. Ordinarily such a personal quality would be considered a gift. In the situation with Debbie, it had been an impediment. The Albertsons had endured repeated disappointments, upsets and embarrassments because of Debbie. Many times they had rearranged their lives in order to please Debbie. No matter how they strived to get her a job or get her into school or pay her bills, Debbie continued to disappoint, upset and embarass them. Her drinking continued. And her addiction progressed. The Albertsons seemed to have such a high tolerance for frustration.

At times, it has occurred to me that it almost would be easier for parents to have a limited capacity for frustration. When their tolerance for frustration is limited, their capacity for intervention can be maximized. For at some point, they more readily can commit themselves to confrontation of the adolescent. If we could monitor their thoughts, they might be similar to the following:

> We have suffered enough because of you. We are not willing to put up with any more. We have done what we can, and what we have done has not helped. We no longer know what to do. *We* need help, too. We cannot go on like this.

Debbie grew up in an age of instant everything. Lights came on with a click of the switch. There was hardly ever a wait for a hamburger at a fast food restaurant. And she could talk long distance within seconds. It was difficult for Debbie to comprehend that therapeutic consultation was not a rapid process. Very often in the course of treatment, Debbie would say:

"How much longer do I have to come here? When will we be finished? Didn't we do this last time? This has been going on for months now. It's been dragged out too long. With all you want to do, this will take a year. That's ridiculous."

Or there were times within a session when she jumped to conclusions with hardly any apparent thought process involved. Impulsive response seemed to reign supreme. Debbie would snap:

"Well, I'm not going to do that any more.
That's not what I meant.
I don't care anyway.
So what if I drank last night. At least I didn't get arrested.
Can I come twice a week to get this over with sooner?
This is all so boring. You just keep saying the same things over and over again. It's stupid."

In the initial phases of treatment, if parents still are caught in a web of denial, their impulsivity often parallels that of the adolescent. At this point, it is common for parents to express their annoyance at the length of the process. If they do not talk with the counselor directly, they will say something to the adolescent. The following comments are examples of parents' limited capacity to proceed at a moderate pace.
To the adolescent:

"Are you still going to that place?
How much longer do you have to go for counseling?
Can't you finish early today? I'm getting tired of waiting.
Will they ever let you have your license back? How long has it been anyway?"

39

To the counselor:

> "Come on, sir, you can't keep my daughter there forever. If this goes on much longer, I'll call my lawyer."

Debbie's addiction to alcohol was advanced enough to result in obvious mental mismanagement. Her view of reality was distorted by alcohol. Although she was intelligent, her harmful relationship with alcohol blurred her ability to make intelligent decisions on her own behalf. With alcohol she felt strong; with the counselor she felt powerless. With alcohol she believed she could handle anything; with the counselor she was uncertain about what she could handle. With alcohol she had a good time; with the counselor she was miserable.

In order to accept her alcoholism, she needed to make a decision. In order to make that decision, her internal conflicts about alcohol needed more resolution. In order to come to a resolution, Debbie really needed to be alcohol-free. She needed to be alcohol-free so that she could listen to what was happening to her. She needed to be alcohol-free so that she could make choices on her own behalf. She needed to be alcohol-free so that she could learn who she really was. Without freedom from alcohol, Debbie's capacity to make a clear decision on her own behalf was minimal.

It is difficult for any adolescent, in an early stage of human development, to make clear decisions. Alcohol complicates that process. In too many instances, alcohol robs the adolescent of the power of free choice and insightful, intelligent decision-making. The ugliness of the disease is that the adolescent does not even realize that her freedom of choice and her capacity for decision-making are no longer available to her.

Impairment of parental capacity to make a decision is influenced primarily by the severity of the adolescent's addiction. If parents have been ravaged by the inappropriate, destructive and unpredictable behaviors of an adolescent whose addiction is advanced, they experience much personal anguish. This anguish is shaped by their own confusion, frustration, guilt and feelings of powerlessness. The strength of this anguish is such that it immobilizes parents who ordinarily are able to function quite well. The confusion, frustration, guilt, and powerlessness which shape parental anguish also destroy or at least seriously weaken parental capacity to make a decision. Decision flows from clarity. Some parents know only the blur of confusion. Decision flows from expectation. Some parents know only the frustration of repeated disappointment and disillusionment. Decision flows from freedom and the reassurance of alternatives. Some parents know only the bondage of guilt and the despair of powerlessness.

The adolescent's and parents' limited capacity to listen, to tolerate frustration, to proceed at a moderate pace and to make a decision are great hurdles en route to an acceptance of alcoholism. Truly, they are barriers to acceptance. However, they are not impassable barriers nor insurmountable hurdles. In fact, they might even be considered advantages. For in order to penetrate these barriers and jump these hurdles, adolescents and parents need to learn more about themselves and about the skills they need in order to cope with alcoholism and recover from it. Such knowledge may come about only because the barriers to acceptance existed. Such knowledge may only become a reality as the barriers are crossed. And so, that which originally was a barrier can serve as an advantage with an improved and more comprehensive view of oneself, others and the situation.

Indications of Acceptance

It must be obvious from the preceding section that the movement to acceptance is a lengthy process. I wish I could offer a secret formula or detailed guidelines for acceleration of anyone's acceptance of alcoholism. But I do not know of such a formula or detailed guidelines. I know only of the length and frustration, the challenge, hope and mystery of the process. I know that acceptance cannot be clocked. Movement to acceptance is not in a linear time frame. Movement to acceptance is in the realm of mystery. Acceptance is born when it is ready to be born. As a clinician, I participate in the readying. And so, I offer you my observation about some of the indications of an adolescent's and her parents' acceptance of alcoholism.

Listening is a skill, an art that can be developed. With the addicted adolescent, true listening can only begin without alcohol. With alcohol, senses are dulled. With alcohol, perceptions become misperceptions. With alcohol, the addicted adolescent cannot enter into herself or into life. At least she cannot make that entrance with any level of awareness, clarity, or creativity. Alcohol robs her of the joy and pain of even hearing her own heart let alone the heart of the world around her. Alcohol robs her of the ability to focus, the ability to concentrate on herself or the world.

An increased ability to listen is crucial for an acceptance of alcoholism. There are two significant aspects to the listening: surrender and concentration, or if you prefer, letting go and focus. Surrender (letting go) implies an ability to give oneself over without resistance. Concentration (focus) implies an ability to pay attention without distraction.

Surrender: The decisive indicator that the adolescent has begun to listen is the fact that she begins to give herself

42

over to the counselor's suggestions. In other words, the adolescent begins to implement counselor suggestions. Such implementation is not simply a grudging compliance but a sincere execution; not just a vague willingness with some inner doubts, but a solid conviction. She now believes she has alcoholism and is willing to do what she needs to do to recover from it. She gives herself over to recovery without resistance.

You may be thinking, "That's all well and good. But how will I know that she listens and gives herself over to her alcoholism and her recovery from it without resistance?" Therefore, I include the following as some significant indicators:

1. change of attitude
2. a. more attention and receptivity within a counseling session
   b. willingness to listen
   c. ability to learn without being argumentative and/or hostile
3. change in inappropriate behavior substantiated by parents, friends, relatives, school personnel or work companions
4. longer periods of abstention from alcohol which are confirmed by reliable sources
5. a sense of peace
6. active participation in A.A. and/or other appropriate self-help groups
7. acknowledgment and performance of responsibilities
8. growth in self-understanding
9. ability to laugh at self
10. notices more of the beautiful world around her
11. ability to have fun without alcohol
12. more accurate perceptions of life situations

13. concern about going to parties where alcohol is in abundance
14. concern about being with friends who drink heavily.

Concentration: For some time, the addicted adolescent hears a distressing conflict within herself. She hears the fight between the desires of her drinking and nondrinking self. At times, these two selves cause her great confusion. She hears the rumblings become a constant clatter in an uproar of confusion. The adolescent really cannot concentrate on this conflict until she has stopped drinking. Until she has stopped drinking she cannot even focus on the counselor's repetitive externalization of this conflict.

At some unpredictable point, however, it becomes clear that the adolescent not only is aware of the conflict, but also is able to focus on it. She is aware and able to express a dynamic similar to the following:

"My drinking self shouted out so loudly that I couldn't even hear a nondrinking self. I wasn't even sure it existed anymore. When my drinking self was in charge of me, I couldn't wait to drink. When my drinking self was in charge of me, I blocked out what you said. Or at least I tried to block out what you said. I didn't want to do anything you told me to do. And lots of times, I wouldn't do anything you told me to do. I thought, I'll show her who's in charge here. She can't tell *me* what to do. There's nothing wrong with me anyway.

"But one day, I heard a different voice inside me. It was a tiny voice urging me not to drink. It was easy for me to shut it up. It seemed like such a tiny voice. But somehow, I don't know how, I heard the tiny voice more often. Each time I heard it, it was stronger. It no longer was tiny. And finally, one day, it was stronger and bigger and more certain than the other voice. I didn't want to hear it. I didn't want it to be strong. It frightened me.

"I knew I had to listen. I knew that drinking was bad for me.

44

I knew alcohol was hurting me. But I didn't know how to stop. I was afraid to stop. I didn't know if I could have fun without alcohol."

Obviously, the preceding passage is but a conceptualization of a process.Hopefully, the adolescent is not hearing any voices other than those which are real or those which are her own thought processes. I included the preceding conceptualization simply for the purpose of clarifying a possible intra-psychic dynamic.

When the voice of the nondrinking self matures and is not stunted by alcohol, it no longer assumes a back seat where alcohol is involved. The nondrinking self somehow engages in a more decisive inner combat with the drinking self. In the beginning, the combat is intense and frequent. And it is exhausting. Once the nondrinking self matures, the adolescent listens with new ears. She is able to concentrate. And now she is able to engage in the struggle involved in her cooperation with the reality of her alcoholism and her recovery from it.

How will you know that her concentration has increased? How will you know that she now pays attention without distraction? I include the following indicators, some of which overlap with the indicators of surrender:

1. more attention and receptivity within a counseling session
2. more active participation in a counseling session
3. ability to express in her own words the painful intra-psychic tension between the drinking and nondrinking self
4. increased ability to identify situations which trigger an urge to drink
5. repeated successes in choosing not to drink
6. less impulsivity in making a decision not to drink; when

presented with the choice to drink or not to drink, she *thinks* first and then decides

7. a sense of peace
8. growth in self-understanding
9. increased enjoyment in nonalcohol-related activities
10. increased annoyance at others' ability to drink appropriately followed by increased indifference about others' drinking.

Listening is a skill, an art that can be developed. As is the case with the adolescent, true listening for addicted parents also begins without alcohol. Needless to say, there are some parents for whom life without alcohol does not become a reality. In these situations, alcoholism is a primary disease for more than one member of the family. If that tragedy exists, an increased parental ability to listen just might not occur. However, if we consider a family whose parents either are free of alcoholism or a family which has at least one parent free from alcoholism, the potential for the development of listening is greater.

Parental ability to listen to reality, as it pertains to alcoholism and the adolescent's recovery from alcoholism, can truly blossom in family therapy and in Al-Anon. Again, as is the case with the adolescent, surrender and concentration are the two significant aspects to parental listening. The indications that surrender and concentration have been reached are similar to the indications listed for the adolescent:

1. change of attitude
   a. towards self
   b. towards the adolescent
2. willingness to listen
3. active participation in therapy and/or Al-Anon

4. growth in self-understanding
5. a sense of peace
6. increased understanding of alcoholism
7. increased detachment from the pain caused by the alcoholism
8. increased ability for focus on self
9. increased willingness and capacity to enjoy ordinary happenings
10. increased ability to learn from listening to others — receptivity to other's input.

And so, at some unappointed time, it is possible for both adolescent and parents to become more attentive and receptive to the demands of alcoholism. This attention and receptivity, in combination with an increased capacity for surrender and concentration, enable the adolescent and parents to be more cooperative in the recovery process. Such attention, receptivity, surrender, and concentration are strong indicators of an acceptance of the disease of alcoholism.

When an adolescent is in the later stages of her involvement with alcohol, the only way she can tolerate any frustration is with a drink in hand. Once she accepts her alcoholism, frustrations do not go away. However, her ability to handle frustration changes.

When she accepts her alcoholism, the following occur:
1. a. growth in her ability to identify what frustrates her
   b. ability to identify real and not imagined frustrations
2. growth in her ability to express her frustrations
3. willingness to learn how to cope with frustrations without alcohol
4. willingness to seek support from others
5. willingness to learn from mistakes

6. a. increased awareness that frustrations will continue
   b. ability to verbalize this fact.

When the preceding changes are observed, the adolescent has crossed another barrier en route to an acceptance of alcoholism. As a matter of fact, such changes indicate that the adolescent's acceptance of alcoholism and her recovery from it are becoming more certain. She has fewer doubts about her addiction to alcohol. She is more convinced that she has a chronic disease.She is more confident, not complacent, that she can recover.

As I indicated earlier, parental high tolerance for frustration can enable an adolescent to continue to drink. That which I focus on now does not contradict my earlier observations. For once parents accept the adolescent's alcoholism, their ability to tolerate the frustration involved in learning begins to increase. There is so much for them to learn about alcoholism and about their own role in recovery. There is so much for them to learn about their own recovery as persons who love an alcoholic adolescent. There is so much to learn.

And learning involves excitement and anxiety, surrender and reconstruction. Learning involves the excitement of acquisition, the realization of new knowledge and the attainment of new skills. In pursuit of knowledge and skill, parents also sustain the frustration which results from the insecurity of unresolved problems or time restraints.

Learning involves the anxiety of self-doubt. It entails not a mere expansion of awareness but often a dynamic internal struggle to understand and to actualize new ideas. Often, the question of capability is raised by even the most skilled parents. In that question lies further frustration.

Learning demands surrender and reconstruction. It requires the surrender of inadequate information which had been perceived as adequate. It requires the surrender of ineffective procedures which had been used in desperation. It requires the surrender of misperceptions which were considered accurate. One of the frustrations of surrender is the reconstruction which can follow. For the process of reconstruction embraces learning and excitement, anxiety and surrender, and even more reconstruction. And so, for many parents, the frustration will lie in the process of a learning that continues to go on and on and on.

Once parents accept the adolescent's alcoholism, their ability to tolerate this frustration increases. At the same time, they are able to learn even more, can endure more frustration and can also continue to develop their own coping skills.

The impulsivity of many adolescents does not come to an abrupt halt. Impulsivity flourishes in insecurity. It is nurtured by its own frequent occurrence. It gains momentum once it is in operation. Time, experience and adequate guidance can help adolescents temper impulsive behavior but cannot eliminate it. One of the many challenges which adolescents face is learning how to use the energy of their impulsivity in appropriate ways.

Once an adolescent accepts her alcoholism, she begins to proceed at a more moderate pace when making decisions to drink. What often occurs is similar to the following:

1. The adolescent is faced with a decision to drink or not to drink.
2. a. She stops to think first.
   b. She considers what has happened in the past.
   c. She considers what a drink will do for her.
   d. She considers what a drink will take away from her.
3. And *then* she makes a decision.

Impulsivity no longer reigns supreme. The adolescent is more aware than ever before that she does have control over some aspects of her life. She might be powerless over alcohol, but she can control her own thoughts about alcohol. She might be powerless over alcohol, but she can make her own decisions about choosing to drink or abstain. And so, when she accepts her alcoholism, the following occur:

1. When faced with a choice to drink or not to drink she chooses not to drink.
2. Within a counseling session she begins to implement the principle of — "Stop and think first before making a response."
3. She applies this principle in other life situations.
4. She expresses feeling more in control of her thoughts and her decisions about alcohol.
5. She feels more self-confident.
6. She is more patient with herself and others.

Such changes indicate that the adolescent's acceptance of alcoholism and her recovery from it are becoming more certain. Because she now believes she has the chronic disease of alcoholism, she continues to choose what she knows is best for her recovery.

I cannot emphasize enough that if parents reject involvement in family therapy and/or Al-Anon, they might reach only a superficial acceptance of the adolescent's alcoholism. Their chances of reaching a solid level of acceptance are enhanced by family therapy and/or Al-Anon. For both family therapy and Al-Anon enable parents to learn how to slow down and care for themselves. Parents who have been ravaged by the adolescent's alcoholism also can be helped by discussion of some of the Al-Anon slogans: Think, Easy Does It, First Things First, One Day at a Time. One of the fruits of focus on these particular slogans is an increased ability to proceed at a moderate pace.

If parents have accepted the adolescent's alcoholism, the following occur:

1. Parents begin to stop and think before making a response to the adolescent.
2. Parents, too, implement this principle of stop and think in other life situations.
3. They become more realistic about what they expect during the adolescent's recovery and their own recovery.
4. They become more aware of their own ability to have control of their thoughts.
5. They are not in a state of panic as quickly or as frequently as in the past.
6. They are more patient with themselves and others.

And so, as parental acceptance of the adolescent's alcoholism matures, their ability to put the brakes on their own impulsivity increases. Now they not only have awareness of the lengthy process in which they and the adolescent are involved but also have accepted that lengthy process as necessary.

The longer an adolescent chooses to stay sober, the more real her view of reality becomes. Her mental mismanagement lessens. Her conflicts about alcohol come to resolution. And her ability to make choices on her own behalf increases, and those choices become more frequent and more significant. When this ability develops, joy and relief charge the adolescent, parents and the counselor.

It is a challenge for any one of us to make repeated decisions on our own behalf. This ability is complex. At the heart of the ability is a profound sense of self. Self-knowledge includes knowledge of what I want and do not want, knowledge of what I can and cannot have, knowledge of what I can and cannot do. Such knowledge is unavailable to an adolescent who is drinking or drunk.

The ability to make a decision on her own behalf also involves an awareness of choices. Simple? Not at all. Choice of point A means rejection of point B. What if both have strong appeal? Tension results. And so, the ability to make a decision on her own behalf means she may experience tension. She is very sensitive to tension. To sustain the tension of decision without alcohol is another sign of her growth.

When the adolescent makes repeated and authentic decisions on her own behalf, it is clear that she is well involved in her recovery. She now is committed to herself and her maintenance of good health. What we see is the following:

1. more ability to identify wants and needs
2. more ability to sustain tension without alcohol
3. choices made which help her maintain sobriety
4. more creative independence.

As parents continue to accept the adolescent's alcoholism, the quality of their decision-making changes. For one thing, they are less likely to make any major decisions while they are upset. They also are less likely to depend on friendly advice from well-meaning persons, persons who often have only limited knowledge of alcohol and alcoholism. They are less likely to take drastic actions in distressing situations. They weigh alternatives and when necessary, consider whether any radical changes will benefit themselves or the adolescent.

What we see occur is the following:

1. Parents permit the adolescent to make decisions and to reap the fruits or suffer the consequences of the decisions.
2. When necessary, parents consult with persons who understand alcoholism.

3. Parents feel more confident about their own decisions.

4. They no longer rush in to rescue the adolescent.

No longer are they bound by their own confusion, disappointments and disillusionment. No longer are they immobilized by powerlessness. They are free to make choices and sometimes even to make mistakes. But they are free.

PART THREE

WHAT HAPPENED TO DEBBIE?

Acceptance is the final stage that adolescents and parents go through when they react to the diagnosis of the adolescent's alcoholism. It is perhaps the most mysterious and difficult stage of all. Some adolescents die alcoholic deaths before they reach acceptance. Other adolescents and parents reach a stage of complete acceptance. And still other adolescents and parents wrestle at length with the initial phases of acceptance. Such was the case with the Albertsons. Let me return to what happened to Debbie and her parents.

In describing what happened, I wish I could tell you about all kinds of wonderful transformations. The fact is, that what I say is quite ordinary, at times discouraging, and always very real. One of the challenges for each of us is to go beyond appearances and to reach for the belief that some kind of significant movement has occurred. I give this preliminarily, because what I now relate might discourage you.

A few days after I shared my diagnostic assessment with the Albertsons in their own home, Mrs. Albertson called me. By that time, Mr. and Mrs. Albertson had time to think and talk about my shared assessment. Mrs. Albertson stated that her husband had a good outlook about Debbie's alcoholism. Debbie, on the other hand, did not want anything more to do with me. But Mrs. Albertson assured me that Mr. Albertson was talking with Debbie.

After I reassured Mrs. Albertson that Debbie's response

was normal, we ended the conversation. I was somewhat relieved. After all, at least Mrs. Albertson had made the overture in contacting me. After only four days, she had called me first. Her phone call had been a bit of reassurance that the family still was connected with me and still involved in the therapeutic process. Or at least I hoped that was the case.

I had not spoken with Debbie, however. And despite her comment about not wanting anything to do with me, I thought that it was important for me to discuss with her my assessment sharing with her parents and her.

And so, I did just that. Because Debbie still was ill, I went back to her home. Debbie received me very well. As a matter of fact, she almost seemed glad to see me. Her parents were not home so our exchange was very free. It was obvious that Debbie felt okay in my presence. She even was quite honest about her sense of surprise that I had told her parents about her alcoholism. There was no apparent hostility manifested by Debbie. Somehow this attractive, young woman respected me. Somehow she even trusted me. And her struggle to face herself and her alcoholism was quite apparent. It also was apparent that Debbie was struggling not to like me. Terrible confusion turned her inside out. She liked me, and I was the enemy. We parted that evening. I was glad we met. I think Debbie was too.

Weeks went by, and I did not hear from Debbie or her parents. Finally, I wrote a letter to set an appointment. Debbie's mother responded with a phone call. Despite the fact that Debbie "was not happy about coming to that agency" and also "wanted to know how much longer she had to go," she *did* make an appointment to see me.

When Debbie returned, she was limping and had tears in her eyes. She said she had been in an accident last night. She burst out, "I wish I had died." After a few minutes, it was quite obvious that Debbie still was very involved with alcohol. For I soon heard her say, "I can say I *was* alcoholic, but I'm *not* an alcoholic." Double talk? Not really. Debbie was trying to tell me that she had not had anything to drink two weeks ago. And at times, she could have taken a drink but chose not to do so. In her eyes, that was a big difference in her drinking pattern. She was right. In her eyes, *she* no longer was an alcoholic. How she struggled! In her eyes, when she drank, she was alcoholic. But when she abstained, she was not an alcoholic. How difficult it was for her to admit to her powerlessness over alcohol.

Debbie left my office that day, but she stayed in my thoughts. I felt a bit encouraged that she had returned to the counseling process. It was easy to like Debbie and to want to work with her. She was quite likeable, very confused and advanced in her addiction to alcohol.

When I went home that evening, I still was thinking about Debbie. I sat down to relax a bit. It had been a full day. I needed to unwind, so I picked up the evening paper. As soon as I began the second section, bold print caught my eyes. "DRINKING/DRUG CHARGES LODGED."

As I read the account, my session with Debbie made more sense. Of course she was limping. The article recounted her most recent accident and her charges. I finished and threw the paper to the floor. I was angry. Had I missed that article, I think I still might not have known the significant details of her accident. She had not told me she was intoxicated. She had managed to keep that vital piece of information from me. And because of her obvious, physical distress, I had neglected to ask that question. I neglected to ask the very question I usually ask first.

Six days after her accident, Debbie and I met again. I was not sure she would keep the appointment, but she did. I told her I had read the newspaper account of her arrest. She was annoyed, but said that the police had told her not to say anything to anyone.

Debbie had been playing pool in bars and drinking soda for a few weeks. But the night of the accident she had at least six beers, one glass of champagne and two white Russians in a few hours. At least, that is what she recalled. She also had used marijuana.

It is important to know the serious nature of Debbie's legal involvement. Her most recent charges were the following:

1. driving while intoxicated
2. driving while her license was revoked
3. switched plates
4. uninsured vehicle
5. unregistered vehicle
6. possession of more than 200 grams of marijuana

This was her third drinking-driving offense within one year. Her first two driving arrests were one week apart and were considered Driving While Impaired (D.W.A.I.) charges.

Debbie knew she was in trouble. She recalled that the public defender told her she could get three months in a county jail, one year in prison, or three years revocation of her license and a $200 fine. Although I had not spoken with the public defender, I too knew Debbie was in trouble.

Mrs. Albertson called me the very next day. She said that she had known nothing about Debbie's arrest until the story "hit the papers." She continued: "The officers suggested that Debbie go to a nearby agency. We have made an appointment for her. Debbie seems to be willing to go there."

I cautioned Mrs. Albertson that Debbie might be trying to manipulate all of us. Mrs. Albertson could not receive my message. For she believed that in the past two weeks, Debbie's attitude had changed. Mrs. Albertson ended with, "It's a big improvement for Debbie."

When I put the receiver down, I was annoyed. Mrs. Albertson would not listen to me. If Mrs. Albertson would not listen, I was certain Debbie would not. Many thoughts were jumbled together all at once. "Don't they see what she's doing? Can't they understand how serious this is? Don't they know that Debbie is running scared? Of course, her attitude is changed, she's scared to death."

Such change needs to be monitored and guided. So often adolescents stop drinking because they are afraid. So often the fear subsides and the change or desire to change stops. So often the adolescent forgets the fear and remembers only the fun alcohol allows. One of the challenges for the counselor is to use the energy of the fear as a springboard for a solid decision for sobriety.

When I met with Debbie again, I could tell her attitude to me had changed. Even her body posture was more rigid. She began what seemed like a rehearsed statement, "I'm going to that other place. The cops told me to go and I'm goin'. Once I go there I'm never comin' back here. You can't make me."

In the face of such anger and apparent rigidity, I calmly responded, "Debbie, I can't change your mind. I want you to understand the terms of the legal mandate for you to be here at this agency. I need to receive a letter from your new counselor stating what your course of treatment will be. If I do not receive such a letter, I will be obligated to notify the Department of Motor Vehicles that your nonattendance at this agency is in violation of satisfactorily complying with their original referral to treatment. In other words, if I do not hear from your new counselor, I must notify the Motor Vehicles Department that you have not complied satisfactorily with the motor vehicle laws. If I have to notify them, they have the right to take legal action in your regard."

Debbie was furious. At this point, she had nothing to say. I quickly added the following, "Debbie, if you decide to go to a nearby agency, I would like your written permission to send them an account of my assessment." Debbie responded immediately. "I'm not gonna sign any papers. If you send anything to them without my permission, I'll take legal action." She got up, stormed out of the room and slammed the door after her.

Sometime shortly after that fiery session with Debbie, her mother called me again. Debbie had been drinking during the past weekend, had a blackout and was scared. She said that Debbie admitted that she needed help. Mrs. Albertson had called a nearby hospital and had Debbie admitted to the detoxification unit. She also said that Debbie was doing well with the counselors there. "Debbie was even able to talk about going to a rehabilitation program." Mrs. Albertson and I ended on friendly terms. However, because of the legal technicalities of a motor vehicle mandate, I sent the following letter to the Albertsons:

I have been informed by a representative of the Department of Motor Vehicles that unless I receive a letter sent to me from a nearby agency which documents Debbie's course of treatment there, I must notify Motor Vehicles that Debbie is in violation of her original referral to treatment at this agency. If I receive such a letter by November, 20, _____, I will not be obligated to notify Motor Vehicles that Debbie is in violation of the original referral. Hopefully, I will receive such a letter with the needed documentation from _____ . Thank you for your cooperation.

Sincerely,

Ann Marie Krupski,
M.A., CAC

I gave the letter two days to reach its destination, and then I called the Albertsons. Mr. Albertson said they had received the letter and would take care of the matter. He also related that they had taken Debbie to a rehabilitation program in a nearby city. Because they were appalled at the reception Debbie received, they took her right back home. When they called Debbie's counselor, he suggested another facility. All of the Albertsons decided against going to another facility. Debbie said she was doing "okay." And Mr. and Mrs. Albertson were pleased that she was going to A.A. To date, however, they had not gone to any Al-Anon meetings.

On November 19, _____ , I received a letter from Debbie's new counselor. Her parents had responded to the letter I sent them. They did not want Debbie to experience the legal difficulty which could result from a violation of the Department of Motor Vehicles orders. Neither Debbie nor her parents had the energy or the finances for another court appearance.

I did not hear from Debbie or her parents again. After the transition of Debbie to the new counselor, I really did not expect to hear from them. I still was uncomfortable that Debbie had refused to give me her written consent to send my assessment and clinical observations to her new counselor. I was uncomfortable because it was obvious that Debbie did not want her new counselor to know what I had observed about her. And that dynamic concerned me. All of her defenses now were operative. Moreover, such resistance about the transfer of information was indicative of Debbie's anger and her use of power.

Her anger: At this point, she was angry that I knew so much about her. She was furious to think that I would be able to give someone else that information. What would the new counselor think? Even more important, what would the new counselor suggest?

Her power: Debbie often had felt powerless in the therapeutic setting. It seemed to her that I almost could read her mind. For I often was able to anticipate many of her responses. And then when I offered an interpretation of what was going on inside of her, she could hardly believe it. What power she gave me. In her eyes, I had it all! So often my interpretations were right on target. And my being on target also angered her. How was I able to know so much about her? How was I able to know what was going on inside of her?

Her refusal to sign a written consent for me to transfer information to a new counselor did not surprise me. However, it concerned me very much. Debbie was intelligent. Indeed, she had the right to refuse to give me written consent. Her response was angry and power-filled. She perceived her response as a chance to get even with me. I perceived it as a predictable challenge for myself. She perceived her response as a chance to escape facing herself and her alcoholism. I perceived it as an escape also. She perceived her response as a chance to exercise her power. I perceived it as a glaring display of a struggle for independence and control. She was trying to manipulate circumstances to her liking.

She already had manipulated her parents. Her plea for help had convinced them of her sincerity. They were unable to see that she was responding out of fear only. They were unable to see that she wanted help only on her own terms. They were unable to see that she had not yet committed herself whole-heartedly to recovery.

And of course, they could not see. They knew very little about alcoholism and thus far had not been able to seek out more information. Of course, they were encouraged. Debbie had never asked for help before. Now she had. She had asked for help on her own. They did not even have to fight with her about it. She wanted to go to the nearby agency. And before, she had not wanted to see me. Of course, they were encouraged. In their eyes, she really had changed. In their eyes, she now was cooperative with the recovery process.

In a few of my many phone calls to the Albertsons, I had described Debbie's ability to manipulate them and others. My descriptions seemed to fall on deaf ears. My message could not compare with the encouragement they felt. They felt a positive response to Debbie's apparent changes. Manipulation did not make sense to them. I was wrong. How could I know? After all, they knew Debbie better than I did.

And so, Debbie's refusal to sign a written consent for me to transfer information about her to a new counselor concerned me very much. However, I was unable to change her mind. She had not even given me a chance to do that. Just as she had slammed my office door, she also had slammed shut her receptivity to my input. Although her parents had not shut out my input so violently, they too blocked my recommendations. And I also was unable to change their minds about Debbie's present course of action.

Ten months after I opened Debbie's case, I closed it. She and I had met twelve times. I had met with her parents on three separate occasions and had more than two dozen phone conversations with them. When I put her file in the cabinet, I was a bit sad. I was sad because I had a sense that Debbie was still manipulating her parents. Debbie had managed to stay out of a rehabilitation program which would afford her a solid structure for learning how to live a sober life. And I was sad because her parents had not yet availed themselves of anything but minimal therapeutic consultation. Nor had they experienced the support of Al-Anon.

Eight months after I closed the case, I had long forgotten the sadness I had experienced. On one very ordinary work day, I received a letter from a probation officer in a nearby city. Attached to the letter was a written statement, signed by Debbie, granting her consent "to release any and all of Deborah Albertson's records to the nearby County Probation Department." Debbie had been arrested again and was under a pre-sentence investigation.

I sent my assessment and treatment recommendations to the probation officer. But I cannot tell you what happened as a result of the investigation and my letter because I do not know. Debbie's case is a closed one on my case list. Her file is terminated. My work with her is finished. My experience with Debbie afforded me new awarenesses about what goes on inside the adolescent alcoholic. I believe that somehow Debbie arrived at new awarenesses about her relationship with alcohol. I believe her parents did, also. At least, I hope so.

There is much darkness inside the adolescent alcoholic and her parents. And where there is much darkness, there is great space for light. I was part of this space creation for Debbie and her parents. And somehow, they were part of a space creation for me.

BIBLIOGRAPHY AND SUGGESTED READING

Breault, William. *Under the Fig Tree*. Notre Dame, Indiana: Ave Maria Press, 1980.

Hesse, Hermann. *Demian*. New York: A Bantam Book published by arrangement with Harper and Row Publishers, Inc., 1965.

Hesse, Hermann. *Steppenwolf*. New York: A Bantam Book published with Holt, Rinehart and Winston, 1969.

Holmes, Donald J., M.D. *The Adolescent in Psychotherapy*. Boston: Little, Brown and Co., 1963.

Jersild, Arthur T. *The Psychology of Adolescence*. New York: The MacMillan Co., 1963.

Kubler-Ross, Elisabeth. *On Death and Dying*. New York: MacMillan Publishing Co., Inc., 1969.

LaFountain, William. *Setting Limits*. Center City, Minnesota: Hazelden Educational Materials, 1982.

Leaton, Kinney. *Loosening the Grip*. St. Louis, Missouri: C. V. Mosby Co., 1978.

Madow, Leo, M.D. *Anger*. New York: Charles Scribner's Sons, 1972.

Marshall, Shelly. *Young, Sober & Free*. Center City, Minnesota: Hazelden Educational Materials, 1978.

May, Rollo. *The Courage to Create*. New York: A Bantam Book published by arrangement with W.W. Norton and Company, Inc., 1975.

Practical Approaches to Alcoholism Psychotherapy. Ed. by Sheldon Zimberg, John Wallace, and Shelia Blume. New York: Plenum Press, 1977.

Stearns, Frederic R., M.D. *Anger/Psychology, Physiology, Pathology*. Illinois: Charles C. Thomas Publisher, 1972.

Svendson, Roger and Tom Griffin. *Student Assistance Program.* Center City, Minnesota: Hazelden Educational Materials, 1981.

Tiebout, Harry M., M.D. "The Act of Surrender in the Therapeutic Process." Distributed by National Council on Alcoholism, Inc., New York, New York.

Tiebout, Harry M., M.D. "Surrender Versus Compliance in Therapy." *Quarterly Journal of Studies on Alcohol*, Vol. XIV, No. 1, March, 1953, pp. 58–68.

Tiebout, Harry M., M.D. "The Ego Factors in Surrender in Alcoholism." *Quarterly Journal of Studies on Alcohol*, Vol. XV, December, 1954, pp. 610–621.

Other titles that will interest you...

When A Bough Breaks
by Mary Ylvisaker Nilsen

A poignant novel that will touch the heart of anyone who has a chemically dependent family member. *When A Bough Breaks* follows a family through a five day family treatment program and relates the dramatic changes they experience. Of special interest to teens, parents, children of alcoholics, and anyone who has been through a family program.
(220 pp.)
Order No. 5090

Enabling Change
by Jane Nakken, C.C.D.P.

Here is real help for the parent whose adolescent child is returning home from treatment for chemical dependency. As the companion piece to *Straight Back Home*, a pamphlet written for the returning adolescent, *Enabling Change* offers compassionate guidance for parents who want to rebuild trust and discover new ways of relating to their child in order to help the family move up the road of recovery together. (24 pp.)
Order No. 1271

Families, Alcoholism and Recovery
Ten Stories
by Celia Dulfano, M.S.W.

Family systems counseling theory is interspersed with illustrative case studies to create an informative guide for those who counsel and treat alcoholics and their families. (163 pp.)
Order No. 1033

For price and order information please call one of our Customer Service Representatives.

HAZELDEN EDUCATIONAL MATERIALS

(800) 328-9000   **(800) 257-0070**   **(612) 257-4010**
(Toll Free U.S. Only)   (Toll Free MN Only)   (AK and Outside U.S.)

Pleasant Valley Road • Box 176 • Center City, MN 55012-0176